THE **DEFENDANT'S** GUIDE TO **DEFENSE**

THE **DEFENDANT'S** GUIDE TO **DEFENSE**

MISDEMEANOR EDITION

CHARLIE ROADMAN

Copyright © 2019 Charlie Roadman

All rights reserved.

No part of this book may be reproduced, or stored in a retrieval system, or transmitted in any form or by any means, electronic, mechanical, photocopying, recording, or otherwise, without express written permission of the publisher.

Published by Right Thing Right Time, Austin, Texas
www. roadmanlaw.com

Edited and designed by Girl Friday Productions
www.girlfridayproductions.com

Editorial: Dan Crissman, Kristin Carlsen, Michael Townley
Design: Paul Barrett
Image Credits: cover © Shutterstock/Inked Pixels

ISBN (Paperback): 978-0-578-54532-5
e-ISBN: 978-0-578-54687-2
Library of Congress Control Number: 2019910894

First Edition

Printed in the United States of America

CONTENTS

Introduction 1

1. Let's Talk About Your Case 5
2. The Courtroom Players 19
3. Following the Rules of the Court................ 57
4. The Best Defense: Make a Plan, Do the Work, and Document It................................ 71
5. The Best Result: Dismissal, Plea Bargain, or Jury Trial? 95
6. Now Is the Perfect Time 131

INTRODUCTION

Have you been arrested for a misdemeanor charge? Is it causing you a lot of anxiety?

I can help. I've represented thousands of people during my career as a defense attorney, and I can explain how the system works in a way that is easy to understand. More importantly, I can explain why it works the way it does and why it is important for you to use this experience to make positive changes in your life.

In this book, I describe the stages of a criminal case, the characters involved, the nuances of negotiating with the prosecutor, and what you can do to help your attorney during the progression of the case. The principles and concepts I discuss will be common in all criminal courts regardless of where you live. However, this book is not about the law itself, which is different in every state. You will have to rely on your attorney for answers to questions about the law specific to your case. But even if you don't yet have an attorney, this book can help prepare you for the road you're likely to face ahead.

> **IMPORTANT**
>
> Show your attorney this book. Most attorneys will be thrilled that you are interested in the judicial process and how you can help.

I wrote this book because defense attorneys do not always have time to spell out the reasons for everything they do. And they often wrongly assume that you already understand the dynamics of the courthouse. This can cause a lot of stress, so I'm going to attempt to solve those issues with this book.

As you read, you'll notice that some of my advice sounds like it should come from a life coach rather than a lawyer. (Note: in this book the terms *lawyer* and *attorney* are used interchangeably.) If this book is about criminal defense, why do I spend so much time talking about making changes in your personal life? It's because I truly believe there is a strong link between your personal development and the outcome of your criminal charge. First, the prosecutors will give you credit for making positive changes in your life. Second, the personal growth will help you emotionally accept whatever the consequences ultimately turn out to be. Finally, the life improvements will reduce the chance that you get in trouble again in the future. Trust me,

I've seen the difference it makes firsthand. And we all have things we can improve, right?

You might be thinking that now is not the time to make significant changes in your life. After all, you've got a case to worry about. But now is the *perfect* time. You have the greatest chance to make real, permanent changes in a critical moment of your life, a time of *peak stress*, such as immediately following an arrest. Perhaps you've already heard the voice in your head saying "It's time to fix this problem" or "I need to start doing this and stop doing that." In other words, your subconscious is ready for change. The moment that tips the scale toward action—the gentle push that starts the process of change—could come from a friend, an attorney, a quote, a movie, a piece of art, a judge, or even a book . . .

My hope is that a small change *now* will snowball into fundamental and permanent life improvements that last far beyond the duration of your criminal case. While your initial reaction may be that the arrest is 100 percent negative, you never really know whether there will be an unexpected benefit.

Consider the following two-thousand-year-old Taoist parable that explains what I'm talking about:

There was an old farmer who had worked his crops for many years. One day his horse ran away. Upon hearing the news, his neighbors came to visit.

"Such bad luck," they said sympathetically.

"Maybe," the farmer replied.

The next morning the horse returned, bringing three other wild horses with it. "How wonderful," the neighbors exclaimed.

"Maybe," replied the farmer.

The following day, the old farmer's son tried to ride one of the untamed horses, was thrown, and broke his leg. The neighbors again came to offer their sympathy for his misfortune. "Sad news," they said.

"Maybe," answered the farmer.

The day after, military officials came to the village to draft young men into the army. Seeing that the son's leg was broken, they allowed him to stay in the village. The neighbors congratulated the farmer on how well things had turned out. "What good fortune!" the neighbors said.

"Maybe," said the farmer.

Is your arrest bad luck? Maybe. It could also be a blessing in disguise. Perhaps it is an opportunity to learn new things about yourself that will result in long-term benefits that are greater than the short-term difficulties.

CHAPTER 1

Let's Talk About Your Case

Obviously, I don't know anything about your case. I don't know who you are, where you live, or what you have been charged with. I do, however, know about the dynamics and structure of criminal cases in general.

But first, I want to tell you a story about elementary school.

When I was eight years old, I threw small rocks at a big metal garbage can during recess. There were other kids on the playground, but no one near the trash can.

Eventually, a teacher sent me to the principal's office. I was handed from adult to adult along the way, and with each passing off, the story of my misbehavior must have gotten exaggerated. When I finally reached the principal, he went nuts. He screamed at me, grabbed my arm, and shook me. (If this happened today, he might end up as one of my clients.)

I tell this story to contrast it with the court system. My punishment at school was pretty much immediate. I was just a passive character. I had no opportunity to gather witnesses, complete a class on the dangers of throwing rocks, clean the chalkboard as community service, or gather letters of recommendation from other teachers. I committed the "crime," and fifteen minutes later, I was punished.

In the criminal court system, there is time to organize your defense. This is because the system is designed to be cautious. All parties want to make sure the right person has been arrested, the punishment is appropriate, and all the rules were followed. Specifically, the length of a criminal case allows you and your defense attorney time to do the following:

1. Look for any evidence that helps your case.

For example, it may be necessary to track down witnesses and videos that contradict the police officer's version of the events.

2. Research the law on your case.

The law is constantly changing: politicians add new laws and change old ones, and higher-level judges modify existing laws. Your attorney needs to see which laws apply to your case and become familiar with the current interpretation.

3. Examine the evidence against you.

In order to defend yourself against the charges, you and your attorney need to know what evidence the prosecutor received from the police (or discovered on their own).

4. Determine if you qualify for any special court programs.

Some courts have alternatives to prosecution for first-time offenders, military veterans, or defendants with alcohol or drug issues. These are often called *pre-trial diversion* programs and can result in a dismissal of the case.

5. Gather documents that could influence the prosecutor to be lenient.

A slow-moving legal process gives you time to complete tasks that could persuade the prosecutor to dismiss or reduce your case to a lesser charge. There are many things you can do to try and convince the prosecutor that this was a one-time mistake and that you have learned your lesson. (More on this in the next chapter.)

> **IMPORTANT**
>
> While the case is pending, you must consider the consequences of all of your actions. Anything you do, good or bad, can impact the outcome of the case.

■ THE ARREST

First things first—odds are your case started off with an arrest by police officers, which can be a traumatic experience. It is common for people who have been arrested to continue to replay the event in their minds over and over. This usually results in questions about the behavior of the police officers and their role in the upcoming case.

Therefore, I will discuss some frequently asked questions about arrests, if only to help you move on and let your defense attorney shoulder the burden of thinking about the officers' actions.

> **The police were aggressive and rude when I was arrested. What can I do about that?**

Explain what happened to your defense attorney, pointing out the reasons that you feel like the police were unprofessional or violated your rights. If your attorney feels like an officer crossed the line, he or she may refer you to an attorney who specializes in lawsuits against the police. If your attorney believes the police officer's conduct was within the law, it is probably best for you to let the anger go and focus on what is important right now, which is getting the best result on your criminal case.

In general, I've found that being mad at the police, no matter how justified it may be, is like the Buddhist saying about holding a hot coal in your hand with the intent of throwing it at someone—it only causes pain to you.

IMPORTANT

Representing clients with a criminal charge and filing a lawsuit against the police for violating your rights are two different types of law. Most criminal defense attorneys do not do both.

What if the police officer is completely mistaken about what happened?

Unfortunately, police officers often overestimate their ability to figure out who is lying and who is to blame in certain situations. Hopefully your defense attorney can convince the prosecutor that the police made a mistake in your case. If not, you will need to accept some type of compromise or request a jury trial.

Did the police have enough evidence to arrest me?

The police must have probable cause before they make an arrest. This means that the police must have a reasonable basis for believing that a crime occurred and that you were the person responsible. This is not the same as "beyond a reasonable doubt." The police don't have to be *certain* that you committed a crime. They just need to be confident that you broke the law and have some evidence to support their belief.

What is considered evidence?

Evidence is anything that supports the claim that a crime was committed. It could be statements from witnesses, a photo of the crime scene, or something incriminating that you said. It could even be *the way* you said something—with suspicious pauses that indicate you were being deceptive. The police themselves are considered witnesses in your case. What they claim to have seen and heard is considered evidence.

Evidence doesn't have to prove something. It can be circumstantial.

> **VOCABULARY**
>
> *circumstantial evidence (n):* Evidence pointing indirectly toward someone's guilt but not conclusively proving it.

For example, let's say that a store owner calls the police and says he caught a teenager spraying graffiti on the side of his store. Perhaps the store owner *did not actually see* the kid paint the wall, but the kid could not explain why he was standing near the freshly painted graffiti with wet paint on his hands. The police also find an empty spray can in the dumpster a few feet away. The evidence in this situation is *circumstantial*. It indirectly suggests that the kid is guilty, but does not prove it conclusively. Make no mistake, though: all of the facts in this situation are considered evidence.

What are my Miranda rights? And what happens if they didn't read them to me when I was arrested?

Law enforcement officers are required to advise you of your rights at the time of arrest, using some form of the following statement: "You have the right to remain silent. Anything you say can and will be used against you in a court of law. You have the right to an attorney. If you cannot afford an attorney, one will be provided for you. With these rights in mind, are you still willing to talk with me about the charges against you?" This is called the Miranda warning.

The police are generally required to recite the Miranda warning to everyone they take into custody. However, the police occasionally forget or are too busy dealing with other issues to read the person their rights. This does *not* mean your case will be dismissed.

If the police do not recite the Miranda warning after arresting you but continue to ask you questions, your responses should not be admissible against you in a jury trial. In other words, the jury would not be told about (or hear) your answers to those questions. It is important to note that Miranda rights only protect you from *police questioning you about the crime after you are in their custody (i.e., not free to leave)*. The police can ask you anything they want before that point.

> **IMPORTANT**
>
> If the police read you the Miranda warning, and you waive your right to remain silent (i.e., agree to talk), they are allowed to ask you questions. And yes, anything you say that is incriminating, or even indirectly supports the prosecutor's theory that you committed the crime, will be used against you.

Miranda violations are usually only an issue when there is a jury trial. When the prosecutor is evaluating a case for the purposes of offering a plea bargain, they will consider any statements that you made—even those in violation of your Miranda rights.

Will the police be in the courthouse on my court date?

It is unlikely that the police officers will be in court unless you are scheduled for a trial. The prosecutors don't need the police officers to be present in court, because the offense report (more on this below) will contain all the necessary information, and the police department would prefer that the officers be on patrol (or getting some rest) rather than sitting around the courthouse waiting for your court appearance. The officers would prefer that too.

■ THE OFFENSE REPORT

Most of the information a prosecutor will receive about a case comes from the offense report, which is written by the officers who were involved in your arrest.

When does the officer write the report?

Officers typically write their report either right after they drop you off at the jail or at the end of their shift.

What will the offense report include?

The offense report will include all of the officers' observations about the arrest, including statements from witnesses and any follow-up investigations that were done (if any). They will use any notes or videos they may have made during their encounter with you.

When will my defense attorney receive the offense report?

The prosecutor's policy on providing the offense report will vary in different jurisdictions. Ask your defense attorney when they expect to receive the report.

Am I allowed to read the offense report?

Yes. Your attorney will let you read it if you ask. However, in most jurisdictions, the defense attorney is not permitted to give you a copy.

Will the offense report give my side of the story?

If you talked with the police officers, the offense report should include what you told them. It should also include the reasons why the police did or did not believe your version of the events. The police may note evidence that raises suspicions about someone else or makes your guilt less clear, but if they thought you were innocent, they would not have arrested you.

What if the offense report is incorrect about some facts?

Always point out anything that is incorrect to your attorney. However, during the plea bargain phase, the prosecutor will not care about small discrepancies. For example, if the officer wrote that your shirt was black, but it was actually dark blue, the prosecutor won't think that is relevant. Those types of mistakes could be important in a jury trial, though.

Do the police care if I'm innocent?

Yes, but they know that arresting an innocent person will occasionally happen (because it is not always easy to know who is lying about what). The officers will hope that if they made a mistake, your attorney will be able to get your case dismissed. The police refer to this as "sorting it out in court."

▍THE THREE PHASES OF A CRIMINAL CASE

After the arrest, the judicial part of the process begins. Most criminal prosecutions can be quite lengthy and subject to various twists and turns, but the progression generally moves through three phases:

Phase I: Administrative

The administrative phase is necessary so that the prosecutor's office can file the proper paperwork and court administration can assign you to a court. This happens quickly in some jurisdictions and slowly in others.

Phase II: Discovery and Negotiation

This is when your attorney and the prosecutor examine the evidence and try to come to a plea bargain agreement that is satisfactory to both sides. The negotiation phase typically lasts from three to ten months. Occasionally, difficult cases can drag on for two or three years. This is also when your attorney will look for any reason that evidence should be thrown out because of mistakes by the police.

Phase III: Resolution

The final phase of a criminal case is when you decide whether to accept the plea bargain or have a jury trial. Your attorney will help you make this decision by describing the pros and cons of each option.

But we're getting a little ahead of ourselves. Before moving on, it's worth pausing to discuss the main players in the courtroom, what they do, and what motivates them.

CHAPTER 2

The Courtroom Players

Throughout your case, you will interact with, or observe, various court employees who do different jobs in the courthouse. Your defense attorney, the prosecutors, and the judge have the most influence on the outcome of your case, but even people in more administrative roles can have a big impact. In this chapter, we'll look at each one of these roles in more depth.

■ THE DEFENSE ATTORNEY

Your defense attorney communicates with the judge and prosecutor on your behalf. They represent you during plea bargain negotiations, give you advice, and use their training and experience to minimize the legal consequences of your arrest.

Official goals:

- To get the best possible result on your case, doing everything *ethically* permissible to minimize your punishment (reducing fines, probation length, jail time, etc.)
- To represent you during plea bargain negotiations and trial (if that happens)
- To make sure you understand the court process and legal consequences so that you can participate in your own defense and make the best decisions

Unofficial goals:

- To finish the paperwork, go to lunch, and get home at a reasonable time
- To make a decent living and pay off their law school debts

To get a better sense of what the job entails, let's look at some common questions I hear about defense attorneys.

Why would someone choose to defend people accused of a crime?

A defense attorney's role and philosophy can be summed up in the maxim that it is better that ten guilty people go free than *one innocent person* go to jail.

How do defense attorneys help innocent people by representing guilty ones? They make sure that the police, prosecutors, and judges follow all of the rules—which are designed to punish guilty people while minimizing the chance of accidentally harming an innocent person.

The existence of good defense attorneys forces the police to gather more and better evidence of a person's guilt. Although this makes police work harder, it decreases the chance that an innocent person is accidentally convicted.

Can a defense attorney guarantee what will happen on a case?

No. In fact, a defense attorney will be cautious about predicting the result. Why?

1. Defense attorneys usually don't have all of the facts at the beginning of a case. Even if you are able to tell your attorney exactly what happened during the arrest, there is no guarantee that the police

officer will remember (or report) the incident in the same way that you recall it.
2. The end result of a case can be influenced by the victim (if there is one) and other witnesses. Sometimes the victim is satisfied that the police arrested you—they don't care what happens afterward. Other times, the victim is still furious months later and wants you to be convicted and punished harshly. Without knowing the attitudes of the other people involved, a defense attorney cannot know for sure how the prosecutor will feel about your particular case.
3. It is not always certain which judge and prosecutor will handle the case. Some judges and prosecutors are tougher than others.

What should the defense attorney be able to tell me about my case?

Once they hear the basic facts of your case, they should be able to tell you

1. the worst-case scenario,
2. the best-case scenario, and
3. the likely result.

> **REMEMBER**
>
> A defense attorney can only base their opinions on the facts that are known to them at the time they are discussing the case with you.

I don't want to have a conviction on my record.

Your defense attorney knows that, I promise. Every case may be different, but everyone has the same goals:

- You do not want to go to jail.
- You do not want to be on probation.
- You want the case dismissed.
- You want to pay as little money as possible.
- You want to spend as little time as possible dealing with the case.
- You want everything clearly explained to you as the case proceeds.

It is not necessary to tell your attorney that the result of your case is very important to you. They already know . . . because it is important to every single client.

> **IMPORTANT**
>
> Ask your attorney, "Have you ever had a case like mine dismissed? How did you do it? What did your client do to help?" An experienced defense attorney will know what needs to happen for a case to be dismissed or if it is even possible.

Will my attorney tell me what to do now?

Yes. In addition to telling you what you need to do to comply with the rules of your release, they will tell you what tasks you should do to get a better result on the case. However, as the case progresses, and more facts are known, they may add new tasks or change what they suggest that you do.

> **REMEMBER**
>
> Once you've hired an attorney, you should let go of the anxiety of having a criminal case (as much as you can). You are paying them, in part, to shoulder the burden for you. You should focus on following their advice and making positive changes in your personal life.

What's the best way to motivate a defense attorney?

It is common for people to want defense attorneys to work extra hard on their case. The best way to do that is to be a good client. This means that you should do these things:

- Give the attorney all of your contact information.
- Respond to all communications from the attorney.
- Follow through with the attorney's recommendations.
- Provide all documents requested by the attorney.

- Ask what you can do to improve your case.
- Always show up to court on time.
- Honor your financial obligations to the attorney.

My defense attorney doesn't expect a good outcome on the case. Are they still going to try?

Yes. Just because your attorney isn't optimistic doesn't mean they aren't going to try to get the best possible result. A defense attorney will always look for every way to minimize the consequences. But rather than giving you false hope, it is better for you to hear the truth at the beginning so you have realistic expectations.

Should I ask my defense attorney to try hard on my case?

No. A defense attorney does not need to be asked to try hard. It is better to ask, "What can I do to help my case?"

I don't understand what my defense attorney is trying to tell me.

Lawyers are highly trained communicators; however, they are primarily trained to communicate with *other lawyers*. Unless you've also been to law school, it can be difficult to understand what your lawyer is talking about. Here are a few tips for getting the most out of your attorney-client relationship:

1. Speak up! Don't be shy. Say, "I don't understand what you mean." It's your defense attorney's job to answer your questions and make sure you understand what is happening.
2. Even if you think you know what something means, double-check.
3. Take written notes. If you're still confused after reviewing them, send an email to the defense attorney and ask for clarification.
4. Bring a friend or family member to court dates and meetings with the attorney. Sometimes having another person present can be helpful.

IMPORTANT

Most defense attorneys will give you extra attention if you have a family member with you at meetings or in court. It forces them to slow down and explain things even more clearly.

Why won't my attorney immediately respond to my calls or emails?

If you're feeling anxious about your case, any delay in answering your questions can be maddening. However, a good defense attorney has a lot of clients. This means that they have obligations and responsibilities to judges, prosecutors, witnesses, and court agencies on many different cases. Your attorney must manage all these obligations so that every client's case gets the necessary attention. Unfortunately, this means that your attorney is often working on other important issues and cannot immediately return your calls or emails. Of course, it is fair to expect them to respond within a *reasonable* amount of time. What's reasonable? Two to three business days on average.

> **REMEMBER**
>
> A criminal defense attorney often has to deal with unexpected and urgent legal matters. Sometimes clients need help immediately. This often requires the attorney's office to redirect all of their resources and attention to the unplanned situation. Be patient when trying to reach your attorney.

What is the best way to communicate with my defense attorney?

Here are some general rules:

1. Email is usually better than a phone call. It provides a record of your communication and allows the attorney to answer when it is convenient for them. If you would prefer to talk on the phone, ask them to call you in the email. Include your phone number (even though the attorney probably already has it in their file).

2. When you write an email, be careful and clear with your words. Try to spell everything correctly—it shows that you made an effort, you respect the attorney, and that you are taking your case seriously. The email does not have to be formal. It can be casual and friendly. However, it should communicate that you've thought carefully about your question or request beforehand.
3. Be polite. Make sure that you are not being passive-aggressive (indirectly expressing anger or hostility).
4. Give your attorney at least two or three business days to reply to your call or email. Often, answers to your questions require research, inquiries at the courthouse, or meetings with colleagues. Definitely follow up if you do not hear back after this time frame. Write something pleasant like: "Hello. Just following up on the email I sent on [date]. Thanks!"
5. Be polite to the defense attorney's office staff.
6. You don't always have to talk to the attorney directly. Sometimes the office staff can answer your question.
7. Don't expect your attorney to have every aspect of your case memorized. The details are in their files.

> **IMPORTANT**
>
> When you ask your defense attorney to do something for you, don't assume that it will be easy for them to accomplish. Some tasks that seem like they should be easy are difficult. For example, resetting a court date sounds like it should be easy. However, this often requires permission from the judge, who is not always available.

Is communication with my defense attorney confidential?

Yes. As long as the communication is private (just between the two of you), everything you say will be confidential.

Should I be honest with my attorney?

Yes. When your defense attorney knows the truth, they are better able to protect you from the consequences.

There may be some circumstances where the defense attorney doesn't want to know, but this is rare. Ask your attorney, "How much do you want to know?" If they say "everything," then tell them everything. It is in your best interest.

My defense attorney doesn't understand that my life will be over if I am convicted.

This is not true, and applying pressure to your defense attorney by exaggerating the consequences of a conviction is not appropriate. I promise that your defense attorney already feels pressure to get the best possible result on your case. If you are having serious anxiety about your case, you should consider talking with a professional counselor or therapist. This could be the best decision you make during this process.

How will I know the fee arrangement with my defense attorney?

The defense attorney should provide you with a legal services agreement (a contract) that outlines the obligations and responsibilities of the attorney, how much you agree to pay, and when payments are due.

Will there be hidden fees?

Most defense attorneys will not have any hidden fees. Everything should be made clear in the legal services agreement. However, be aware that the money you pay to your defense attorney will not cover fines, court costs, fees for classes, or other expenses that can be typical in criminal cases.

> **IMPORTANT**
>
> Unlike civil attorneys, criminal defense attorneys do not charge you for every phone call they make and email they answer. Criminal attorneys typically charge a flat fee for legal representation.

What if I get in more trouble while my original case is pending?

Your defense attorney is only responsible for the legal issues that are listed on the legal services agreement. You will likely have to pay another legal fee to the attorney to represent you on any new legal issues that may arise, even if they are related to the original charge.

What if I have a hard time making payments?

Your attorney may withdraw from your case. If that happens, your attorney usually gets to keep all the money that you have paid to date—and then you'll have to go hire *another* attorney. Before you choose a defense attorney and commit to a payment plan, look at all your financial resources—including the possibility of borrowing from family and friends—to figure out exactly what you can afford.

REMEMBER

To get an extraordinary result in your case, your defense attorney must keep fighting for you, even when it would be easier to advise you to take the current plea bargain offer. It is hard for a defense attorney to summon the energy to continue to fight when you are not paying them for their work.

Why are defense attorneys so expensive?

This is what you are paying for:

- Assuming responsibility for your case once hired
- Their experience and knowledge of the law
- Their familiarity with the local court system

Once a defense attorney is retained, he or she will use all of their experience and knowledge to guide you through the legal system. They will review all the evidence and ensure that the police, prosecutors, and judge do not violate your constitutional rights.

If your attorney makes a mistake due to negligence (for example, forgetting to file a motion or not carefully researching the law) they can get in trouble with the state bar association—the government agency that gives an attorney a license to practice law. In other words, every time an attorney accepts a case to handle, they take on pressure, risk, and liability.

> **IMPORTANT**
>
> Defense attorneys also work on cases in between court settings. This includes administrative tasks, researching the law, talking to colleagues, and thinking about possible legal strategies. *You are paying for more than just the time the attorney is at the courthouse.*

What if I can't afford an expensive attorney?

It may be hard to believe, but expensive attorneys do not always get better results. Every year a new group of lawyers graduate from law school. They will be passionate, hungry, and less expensive than their more experienced colleagues. Sometimes passion can get a better result than experience.

Should I hire the aggressive attorney from the TV ad who says he'll "FIGHT!"?

I'll let you in on a little secret. Those "aggressive" attorneys act like normal people at the courthouse. They have to. No one would tolerate defense attorneys acting like pro wrestlers when negotiating a case. Often the attorneys on TV are just being salespeople. This is not bad, of course. Many are great attorneys. But remember, even the calmest attorneys will fight for you.

What if I'm not happy with my lawyer?

If you aren't satisfied with your attorney, you can hire another lawyer. Before you do that, though, talk frankly with your current lawyer to make sure the problem isn't just a communication issue or a misunderstanding. It may feel like your attorney isn't doing anything, but that is often because you aren't aware of all the times when your attorney is thinking about your case, strategizing about how to get the best result. A lack of communication from your attorney does not necessarily mean that he or she is doing a bad job handling your case. It usually means that nothing has changed since the last time you talked to him or her. Ask to have a meeting with your attorney if you are really concerned.

If you're certain you want to get a new attorney, you have the right to hire any lawyer who will agree to take your case (as long as the judge approves the change).

However, as a general rule, the further along you are in the process, the harder it is to switch attorneys.

■ THE PROSECUTOR

In your criminal case, the prosecutor represents the government. Their job is to seek the appropriate punishment for people who violate the law. While their judgment is not perfect, they will not knowingly punish people that they believe are innocent. They are very powerful because their personal opinion of the case often determines (or at least influences) the outcome.

Official goals:

- To administer a fair amount of punishment to you
- To dissuade you from committing a crime again
- To satisfy the victim, if any, that you were punished appropriately
- To make sure that any damage or loss to any parties involved is paid for or taken care of in one way or another
- To show the local community that crime will be punished

Unofficial goals:

- To keep their job
- To be promoted
- To be able to take a lunch break
- To have a reasonable work-life balance
- To pay off their law school debts

Here are some common questions I hear about prosecutors:

Who exactly is prosecuting me?

This can be confusing if there were other people involved in your case. For example, if you are charged with criminal mischief for breaking the window of a store, the store owner is considered the victim. However, it is the state or city that is filing the charge against you. Your case will be titled the **State/City of _____ vs. You**.

Why is that significant?

It is significant because the *prosecutor* will decide whether to be tough on you or whether to be lenient. The prosecutor may seek a victim's opinion about how you should be punished, but ultimately the prosecutor will decide how to handle the case.

Are there different types of prosecutors?

Yes. Some are tough and others are less so.

Do all prosecutors have the same level of authority?

No. Some prosecutors have more authority than others—usually based on how long they've worked in that particular office. A senior-level prosecutor will have the authority to offer better plea bargains than a lower-level prosecutor. However, this does not mean they will.

IMPORTANT

The prosecutor who is handling your case can change. Sometimes there is a different prosecutor every court date. The new prosecutor will look at the notes of the previous prosecutor to know what has been discussed.

What does every prosecutor have in common?

Every prosecutor has a college degree, has been to law school, and has passed the bar exam. They are employed and supported by the government, so they will be confident and have self-respect. They might be persuaded to do something, but not intimidated. All of them believe that the rules we have made for our society should be followed by everyone.

How many cases does a prosecutor handle?

It depends on the size of the jurisdiction. However, some prosecutors are responsible for hundreds of cases at any given time.

How do they remember the details of so many cases?

They don't. They rely on their files—which include the offense report and any notes they've taken about the case. Prosecutors generally review the facts of a case while talking with the defense attorney at each court date. Unless there is something memorable, dramatic, or troublesome about the arrest, a prosecutor will have to refresh their memory about the facts of your specific case before talking with your defense attorney.

Will I talk to the prosecutor?

No. Your defense attorney does that for you.

What if I want to talk to them?

You should ask your attorney if that is possible (or a good idea). But it is unlikely that the prosecutor will want to talk with you. Prosecutors would prefer to deal with defense attorneys.

Will the prosecutor care about all the bad things that have been happening in my life?

Unfortunately, prosecutors regularly hear defendants blame their arrest on whatever was going on in their life before the incident (e.g., they had a tough day at work, they were getting over an illness, they just broke up with their girlfriend or boyfriend). Even when a defendant accepts some responsibility for their behavior, they often still deflect blame to other people or circumstances.

For obvious reasons, prosecutors are much more focused on the incident itself—the part of the story where you broke the law—than what's going on with your life. Anything other than accepting responsibility and making a plan sounds like an *excuse*, and an excuse will actually work against you in the prosecutor's eyes. Here's why: When you say, "It wasn't my fault;

my girlfriend just broke up with me," the prosecutor hears, "Whenever I have relationship issues, I'll probably commit this crime again." This will make the prosecutor think that a dismissal is not the right answer in your case and that you need stiff punishment and a conviction to influence your future behavior.

In other words, the prosecutor will definitely listen to your defense attorney describe the things you are going through, but they will be more interested in the *good things you are doing now* than the bad things that happened to you in the past.

Can my defense attorney choose which prosecutor handles the case?

Sometimes. This is called *prosecutor shopping*. If possible, your attorney will attempt to negotiate with the prosecutor that has the sympathetic personality, confidence, and experience to dismiss the type of case that you have. This practice is generally frowned upon by the prosecutors because they want to believe that the facts of each case are what determine the outcome, not which prosecutor is assigned to the case.

Unfortunately, it is not always possible for the defense attorney to choose which prosecutor handles your case. Often, prosecutors are pre-assigned to specific cases by their boss.

What if the prosecutor is unfair to me?

Your defense attorney will make sure that doesn't happen. If there is a problem, your attorney will notify the judge. The judge will make sure that the prosecutor complies with the rules.

Does it help if the defense attorney knows the prosecutor personally?

A prosecutor won't deliberately offer a better deal to a defense attorney just because they are friends. That is considered unethical, and if the prosecutor were to be caught, they could be fired. Has this ever happened? Sure, but it is not common enough to be a concern.

Will the prosecutor treat VIPs differently than me?

A prosecutor is ethically prohibited from giving anyone special treatment without a legitimate reason. The media provides the best oversight against any tendency to favor certain people over others. Prosecutors do not want to be criticized in the newspaper, on TV, or on the internet. Any critical story could cause trouble for them individually or for their boss.

For example, let's say that the mayor's daughter gets arrested for shoplifting. While a prosecutor might be inclined to go easy on the mayor's daughter, they know the media would certainly point out that she had received special treatment. This could motivate the community to support another candidate for county or district attorney at the next opportunity. The safe bet for a prosecutor is to make sure that the mayor's daughter does *not* get any special treatment.

Would a prosecutor ever let their personal life affect their decisions?

Prosecutors will try not to be influenced by their personal life. However, because they're human, it doesn't always work out. For example, the morning after a prosecutor has a huge fight with their spouse, it could be harder for them to listen sympathetically to a defense attorney. The opposite can also be true. If a prosecutor is in a good mood, they can be more lenient.

A good defense attorney will be able to sense the mood of the prosecutor and adjust their strategy accordingly. Sometimes the best course of action is to wait and discuss important points on a day when the prosecutor is under less stress.

Do police officers influence prosecutors in certain cases?

Police officers generally want prosecutors to be tough on defendants because they believe that harsh punishment is the best way to reduce crime. But, unless there is something unusual about your case, the prosecutor is unlikely to contact the police officer when deciding on the plea bargain offer. This is because the offense report will contain all of the information that the prosecutor needs.

In general, once the police have arrested you, delivered you to the jail, and written their offense report, they consider their job to be done. You are now the responsibility of the prosecutor and judge. Unless the officer has to show up for a trial, they are unlikely to think about you again.

■ THE JUDGE

The judge is the referee of your case. They make sure all the rules are followed. Some judges pay close attention to all the cases on their docket; others only get involved when a resolution has been reached, a problem arises, or the case is set for a jury trial. While your case is pending, the judge will make sure that you are complying with the terms of your release (the bond).

VOCABULARY

bond (n): The legal agreement that releases you from jail and requires you to appear in court. The bond may also have other conditions that you must follow.

If the prosecutor and defense attorney have worked out a plea bargain, the judge will review the terms of the deal and either accept or reject the agreement. If no plea bargain agreement is reached, the judge will oversee the trial.

> **REMEMBER**
>
> Politicians make the law, not the judges. A judge's job is to make sure the law is followed.

Official goals:

- To give you the opportunity to fight the charge against you
- To ensure you are treated fairly and the law is followed by the prosecutors, police, and your defense attorney
- To make sure the amount of punishment is appropriate if you are found guilty
- To assure the community that the criminal justice system is effective and fair
- To satisfy the victim (if there is one)

Unofficial goals:

- To keep their job, by election or appointment

Below are some common questions I hear about judges.

How do judges vary in personality?

There are all types of judges. Some are stern and intimidating. Others are friendly and sympathetic. While the judge's personality will certainly affect your experience, all judges know that their role is to be fair to you.

What power does the judge have over me while the case is pending?

The judge is allowed to set conditions on your bond. For example, they can prohibit travel, require counseling, forbid you from drinking alcohol, set a curfew, add a GPS ankle monitor, or make certain locations off-limits. Your attorney can ask the judge to remove the conditions if there is a good reason; however, the judge would have to agree.

How long will a judge allow my case to go on?

The judge needs to give your defense attorney and prosecutors enough time to gather evidence, research the law, and attempt to negotiate a plea bargain. However, because new cases are constantly being added to their docket, the judge needs older cases to be resolved. If the docket grows too large, the judge won't have enough time to address the issues on cases that need attention. In other words, the judge will attempt to give the defense a fair amount of time, but not so much that it impairs the functioning of the court.

What does the judge consider when making decisions?

Any possibility that something negative could result from a decision will make the judge very cautious. Judges are always thinking about the hypothetical future tragedy—a terrible event that was foreseeable and preventable. If the facts of your criminal case suggest that you are likely to commit another crime, the judge and prosecutor will take precautions by placing restrictions on you while your case is pending.

> **IMPORTANT**
>
> While some aspects of the criminal justice system are designed to punish for past behavior, other elements are designed to protect the community from possible future behavior.

Does the judge care about what happens to me?

Of course. The judge wants the prosecutor, victim, community, and *you* to be satisfied with the outcome of the case. Of course, that is a difficult balance to reach. If it doesn't happen, the judge will be satisfied as long as everyone is confident that the process was fair.

THE COURTHOUSE SUPPORT STAFF

In addition to the judge and the prosecutor, your defense attorney will interact with a variety of courthouse employees while representing you—people with specific roles in the bureaucracy of a criminal justice system. Your attorney must understand everyone's role to make sure that your case is handled correctly. It will be beneficial for you to understand these roles as well.

Here's an overview of the support staff in the courthouse and their goals:

■ THE COURT ADMINISTRATOR

The court administrator is similar to an office manager. They keep track of the court dates, oversee the judge's office, and sometimes act as the gatekeeper to the judge.

The court administrator is neutral about the result of any case.

Official goals:

- To run the court under the judge's direction
- To manage the court's docket
- To answer phones, emails, and faxes, and perform general office management duties

Unofficial goals:

- To get a lunch break and go home at a reasonable time

- To put in enough time to get a pension at the end of their career

■ THE COURT CLERK

The clerk is in charge of the paperwork for each criminal case. The clerk's file includes all documents filed by the prosecutor, defense attorney, and judge. The file is arranged chronologically so that the sequence of events is easy to determine. While you are unlikely to have much interaction with the clerk, it is worth understanding how important their job is. They make sure that everything about your case is recorded accurately. This is important, because if the paperwork isn't accurate, it could cause more problems for you in the future.

> **IMPORTANT**
>
> The clerk's file is public record (anyone can view the documents). The defense attorney and prosecutor will also have files, but those are not available to the public.

The clerk will notify other government agencies that are affected by the result of the criminal case. For example, if your driver's license is suspended by the judge, the clerk will notify the agency in charge of driver's licenses.

The clerk is neutral about the outcome of the case.

Official goals:

- To make sure the paperwork is accurate
- To notify other government agencies about the result of the case

Unofficial goals:

- To finish the paperwork, go to lunch, and get home at a reasonable time
- To put in enough time to get a pension at the end of their career

■ THE COURT REPORTER

The court reporter, also called a stenographer, is in charge of transcribing any important discussions, hearings, or trials. This is required in the event a higher-level court needs to review what happened in your case. However, because the majority of communications between the judge and attorneys are about scheduling and other minor issues, not everything that is said in court will be transcribed.

The court reporter is neutral about the result of the case.

Official goals:

- To accurately transcribe trials, hearings, and important discussions

Unofficial goals:

- To get a lunch break and go home at a reasonable time

■ THE BAILIFF

The bailiff is the security officer for the court. They keep an eye out for potential threats and take directions from the judge on managing the courtroom. They enforce the court's dress code—no hats, shorts, or flip-flops—and ask people in the courtroom to keep the noise down so that the judge (and court reporter) can hear. The bailiff often does some clerical work—for example, calling the docket (taking attendance)—to help the court run efficiently. The bailiff is neutral about the outcome of the case.

Official goals:

- To protect the judge, court staff, attorneys, and everyone else in the courtroom
- To keep everyone in the courtroom quiet and respectful
- To enforce the dress code
- To take people into custody for being in contempt of court or for other rule violations

> **VOCABULARY**
>
> *contempt (n):* Being disrespectful to the judge or not following a lawful order.

Unofficial goals:

- To get a lunch break and go home at a reasonable time

■ THE PROBATION OFFICER

The in-court probation officer represents the probation department in the courtroom. They do the paperwork if you accept a plea bargain that includes probation.

Official goals:

- To explain the rules of probation to you
- To notify the judge if you break the rules of probation

Unofficial goals:

- To finish their work so they can go home

As you can see from the motivations I described, the people that work in the courthouse are primarily concerned with doing their job. They will follow the established rules and procedures of the courthouse and do everything they can to make the process fair to everyone. If you follow the rules too, your case will go much more smoothly.

CHAPTER 3

Following the Rules of the Court

The first step to getting a good result on your criminal case is to follow all the rules while your case is pending. That sounds obvious, right? But it is often harder than it sounds because the requirements can be confusing and the court system does not always explain clearly what you need to do or how to do it. In fact, you might even get contradictory explanations and instructions! It is natural to get frustrated and want to stop trying to comply with the rules and requirements. This is a very bad idea, because eventually the judge or prosecutor will be notified that you failed to follow the rules of the court. They will likely form the opinion that you are not going to follow the rules in the future either.

This will make them assume that stiff punishment is the better result on your case (to influence your future decision-making).

What does following all the rules mean? It means that you do everything you are supposed to do, when you are supposed to do it, no excuses. You must follow every instruction to the letter. In order to comply with the requirements, you may have to reschedule events that have been planned for months, find new transportation options, get a second job, borrow money from friends or family, or adjust your lifestyle according to the new rules. You must do these things! The judge, prosecutor, and court system want you to solve any issues that you run into. Your goal is to be a model defendant, causing no problems at any point during the process.

Following the rules seems like a no-brainer. However, it quite common for some defendants to basically ignore them. They feel like it's their attorney's job to resolve any problems resulting from the criminal case. This is not a good strategy for success. A defense attorney cannot eliminate every requirement that comes with getting arrested.

What if I am slow or fail to complete a court requirement?

If you've been told to do something by the judge or your defense attorney, you should do it ASAP. The court system isn't like high school, where the teachers eventually get exasperated and let you pass without completing the work. Judges, prosecutors, and the justice system in general will not let you avoid requirements by delay and excuses. This will frustrate them and make them more determined to punish you. Your goal should be to impress them with the speed in which you did the tasks!

> **REMEMBER**
>
> The courtroom will be full of people making excuses for why they couldn't do something. Don't be one of them.

What should I do if I'm supposed to do something, but the agency or company won't call me back?

There are often situations where you are required to complete a task, make a reservation, or check in with an agency, but you can't get through or they won't call you back. You must not give up! Keep trying! Even though it is not your fault, you can still get in trouble for not doing what you are supposed to do. Unfortunately, customer service is often not a high priority for government agencies or businesses that work in criminal justice. You should continue to try and make contact on a regular basis. Call every day if necessary. Remain calm and polite, of course. If you run out of ideas, call your attorney and see if they have any advice.

Will the courthouse staff help me?

Whichever agency gave you the paperwork will likely be happy to help you understand it. They aren't going to mislead you in any way, because they want you to comply with the rules. What they won't be able to do, however, is help you solve the problems that make it hard to meet your obligations. You will have to do that on your own.

If there is anything that you don't understand about what you are supposed to do, ask your attorney.

What if I can't pay for the class, monitoring device, or other fee that I'm required to pay?

There is no easy way to say this . . . You just have to find a way. Talk to your family and friends to see if they will help. Sometimes defendants don't do a task because they can't afford $100, but the consequence of not completing the task ends up costing $2,000 over the long run. You must use all of your problem-solving skills to pay for anything ordered by the court.

> **IMPORTANT**
>
> The court system does not care that being arrested makes things difficult for you. In fact, the court will assume that the harder it is on you, the more likely you will be to remember the consequences and, in turn, the less likely you will be to get in trouble again.

■ GOING TO COURT

When the time comes for you to go to court, there are some basic rules to follow that will make the process easier. But first let's acknowledge that it can be frightening to go to court. In part, that is because courtrooms are designed to be intimidating. The architecture of the building (e.g., high ceilings) are purposely designed to create a sense of power and awe. It is not an accident that the judge is elevated high above everyone else in the courtroom. It is natural to feel nervous. But as long as you are following the rules, there is no need to be excessively anxious.

How should you act when you go to court? The rules of the court are established by the presiding judge. In most courts, the general rules will be as follows:

- Show up on time.
- Do not use a phone or computer in the courtroom.
- Do not eat, drink, or chew gum.
- Dress appropriately. Take off your hat.
- Do not read the newspaper (but reading a book is usually OK).
- Stand up when the judge enters the courtroom.

Do I need to come to every court date?

Ask your lawyer. Each judge has their own attendance policy. Some require you to be at every court setting, while others only want you to attend once the case is ready to be resolved.

> **IMPORTANT**
>
> Most courts call the docket when the judge first arrives in the courtroom. This is like taking attendance in school. If you are not there, they will mark you as absent. If you arrive late, try to get a court employee's attention and let them know that you are present. But my advice is don't be late.

Can my attorney change the court date?

Sometimes. However, the judge must approve the change. To increase the chance that the judge will agree, provide your attorney with documentation of the reason you are asking for a new date. For example, if you have an out-of-state work trip, get copies of the flight information or hotel reservation. Requesting a new court date requires your attorney to do extra work, so make sure that the reason you need a new date is important.

> **IMPORTANT**
>
> Do not count on getting your court date changed. Some judges will absolutely refuse to move court dates for your convenience.

What happens if I miss a court date?

If you are late or miss a court date, the prosecutor and judge will come to three conclusions:

1. You don't respect the judge.
2. You don't have common sense.
3. You need to be taught a lesson.

The judge will likely revoke your bond if you do not show up for court when you are required to attend. This means that a warrant will go out for your arrest. If the judge is in a good mood and you have an acceptable reason for missing court, you might be given another chance to appear. However, you should not count on this.

Make sure that you put your court date in your phone calendar and have reliable transportation to the courthouse on your appearance date. Have a plan B,

C, and D in case something unexpected happens. If your car breaks down, call a taxi or ride-share service immediately. Don't count on the judge excusing you from court because of car troubles.

Calling your defense attorney and explaining why you won't be in court is not enough to avoid getting in trouble. The judge must excuse your attendance. To improve the chance that the judge will believe your explanation, you should provide your attorney with proof of the problem (pictures, emails, receipts, etc.). Remember, even proof of a legitimate reason that you cannot attend court will not guarantee that a judge will excuse your appearance.

> **IMPORTANT**
>
> Don't wait until the morning of your court date to figure out where the court is! Look up the court's website on the internet well in advance. The website will have answers to basic questions about location, parking, etc.

I have a family vacation (or work event) coming up. Do I need to tell someone?

Yes. Tell your defense attorney as far in advance as possible. Email them with the dates and description of the event. Include any documentation that shows what you will be doing. Your attorney will let you know if there are any issues with the plans. Remember, whether you are permitted to travel or reschedule court dates is up to the judge, not your defense attorney.

How should I dress for my court date?

The judge sets the dress code for the courtroom. Most judges will be OK with regular clothes, as long as you don't wear shorts, T-shirts, or flip-flops. Take off your hat when you enter the courtroom. Don't wear anything that has branding for alcohol. Ideally, you should wear what you would wear if you were going to a nice restaurant or graduation ceremony. The whole point of dressing up is to show respect to the judge. You do not need to wear a suit, but no one has ever been criticized for doing so.

I don't see my attorney in court. What should I do?

If your lawyer is running late, the court will not hold this against you. Most judges allow the lawyers to appear in court later than the defendants. For example, while you might need to be in court by 8:30 a.m., your attorney can show up anytime between 8:30 a.m. and 11:00 a.m. This is necessary because defense attorneys often have many different obligations each morning.

Also, just because you don't see your attorney in the courtroom doesn't mean they aren't already in the courthouse somewhere. Often the attorneys are working on cases in the back rooms of the courthouse. My advice is to call (or text) your lawyer's office when you arrive in court to politely let them know that you are present.

How many court dates will there be?

Ask your lawyer how many court dates to expect. Remember, this will only be an estimate because there are often unexpected delays. It also depends on the personality of the judge. Some judges pressure defense attorneys and prosecutors to resolve cases quickly—within two to four court appearances. Other judges allow more time to negotiate a plea bargain—sometimes more than twenty court dates! At some point, even the most patient judge will apply pressure to both sides to come to an agreement or set the case for trial.

> **IMPORTANT**
>
> Don't assume that your court date was reset at the request of your defense attorney. Sometimes the prosecutor or judge will require the case to be delayed for their own reasons. If you want to know why your court date was reset, ask your attorney.

I'm frustrated with how my court appearance is going. Should I let a court employee know?

Probably not. Complaining about the court process to the court staff rarely gets a sympathetic response. In fact, complaining generally annoys the court staff and can end up making your experience even less pleasant. My suggestion is to explain your feelings to your defense attorney and get their advice on what can be done.

> **REMEMBER**
>
> The courthouse has rules in place to keep the court running smoothly. The courthouse staff is not going to bend the rules to make the process more convenient for you.

I have to go back to work. Will the judge let me leave early?

No. Because you have advance notice of your court date, the judge will expect you to make the appropriate arrangements with your employer to attend court for as long as necessary. If you don't know how long to plan for, ask your attorney.

> **IMPORTANT**
>
> Let your employer know that you need the morning (or afternoon) off for your upcoming court date. If you don't want to let them know about the case, you can tell them that you need to handle a personal issue.

There will be a lot of waiting around throughout this process, in places like the courtroom, your attorney's office, and various counseling offices. Bring a book, start a journal, make sure your phone is charged. Do not act upset or annoyed. It will not make the situation any better. The best strategy is to *expect* that everything will take a long time. You can even use that time to think about your personal goals and make a plan.

CHAPTER 4

THE BEST DEFENSE

Make a Plan, Do the Work, and Document It

Defendants who want the best chance to get a positive result will go above and beyond the basic requirements in a typical court case. They will set ambitious personal goals and make progress toward reaching them. They will get letters of recommendation from employers, teachers, or mentors. They will apply to college or find a better job, start therapy or deal with medical issues. These are not things that you *have to do*, they are things that *you should do*. This is because prosecutors are *very interested* in positive stories—especially stories about life improvements you have made since the arrest. Positive stories make the prosecutors feel good about the judicial system. They think, "We arrested this person, and they have taken it to heart. The system worked. They are unlikely to get arrested again." We want the prosecutor to be impressed with what you have done while the case was pending.

In order to impress the prosecutor, you need to

1. set personal goals and make plans to achieve them,
2. do the necessary hard work, and
3. provide documentation to your attorney.

Don't wait for the case to be over to make changes in your life. The goals and plans you make now could become a reason that the prosecutor decides to be lenient in your case. It is not easy to do, but that's why it is so valuable when it is done.

> **IMPORTANT**
>
> Do something that you would not have done otherwise. When you look back you should be able to say, "I wouldn't have accomplished this, this, and this, if it wasn't for the arrest."

■ YOUR GOAL IS A STORY

A good story has a hero who must overcome a conflict to reach a goal. In our story, you are the hero, and the arrest is the conflict. The prosecutor is the audience.

The prosecutor needs to know what your goal is. Where are you going in your life? What are you trying to achieve? How will you get past the setback of this arrest?

Showing ambition to the prosecutor serves a couple of purposes. First, it helps them relate to you—after all, becoming a lawyer takes ambition. Second, the prosecutor knows that people moving toward an ambitious goal are less likely to engage in reckless behavior.

You should work with your defense attorney to develop a story that represents your own ambitions. Lay out some practical steps you can take to reach the goal—for example, get a GED, sign up for community college, apply for a new job or promotion, start a new business. Choose something that is challenging. You won't get much credit for doing something that was easy to do. Be ambitious. Do something out of your comfort zone.

Discuss the options with your family, friends, and other people you respect. Create a vision of your future and design a plan to get there. That's your story.

> **IMPORTANT**
>
> Open your mind. Listen to your friends, family, and counselors. Truly consider what qualified and experienced people tell you.

■ DO THE WORK

After you have set your goals and made your plans, the next step is to do the hard work. This means that you begin executing your plan. Start completing the small steps of the journey.

Doing the work may require you to make sacrifices or changes to your daily routines. For example, you might have to spend extra time after work or on the weekends (when you would normally relax). Maybe you should make a pledge to complete parts of the plan before you resume your normal lifestyle?

This is also a good time to focus on exercise and other health-related improvements. Ironically, spending time on feeling better will increase the chance that you'll find time to do the necessary work on your plan.

While it is possible that everything that you do while the case is pending will have no effect on the outcome of the case, in my experience most prosecutors are moved by the actions you take. Sometimes a small thing can reduce the punishment significantly. For example, completing private counseling or getting a few powerful letters of recommendation while your case is pending might reduce the punishment from two years of probation to one year. That would be worth it, right?

The strategy is to choose goals that benefit you regardless of their impact on the case.

■ PROVIDE DOCUMENTATION

Just telling your attorney about your goals and plans isn't enough. Your attorney needs documentation that they can share with the prosecutors. Try to get proof of each step as you complete it. Collect screenshots, receipts, pictures, and any other documentation that proves what you have accomplished.

Do not underestimate the importance of providing paperwork. The prosecutors need to put something in their files to justify a lenient offer. Without the proper documentation, your defense attorney will end up in a situation like this:

Prosecutor: Did your client take the classes?
Defense attorney: Yes.
Prosecutor: Where are the certificates?
Defense attorney: I don't have them.
Prosecutor: How do you know he did the classes?
Defense attorney: He told me he did.
Prosecutor: Really? Come back when you have proof.

Good things that can't be proven on paper aren't worth much in the court system. Unfortunately, too many defendants have made claims that aren't true. Sometimes they will say they have accomplished a task when in fact they have only made plans to eventually do it. For example, this is a common interaction between defense attorneys and clients:

Defense attorney: Did you complete the class?
Client: Yes!
Defense attorney: Great! Let me see the certificate.
Client: Well, the class isn't over yet. I should have it by Friday.
Defense attorney: OK. Let me see the receipt for paying for the class.
Client: Actually, the class hasn't started. It begins tomorrow.
Defense attorney: Hmm. OK. Let me know when you complete it.
Client: Will do . . . Um, what class was I supposed to take again?

Prosecutors know that it is common for defendants to exaggerate where they are in the process of completing tasks. That's why they will only give credit for things that are proven with documents.

THE GOOD GUY / GOOD GAL PACKET

All of the documents that you provide to the attorney will be presented to the prosecutor as a *good guy* or *good gal* packet. This packet is a collection of mitigation documents that show the prosecutor who you are, what you've accomplished, and what your plans are for the future. It is important to give the prosecutor as many reasons as possible to be lenient. You never know which document will tilt the scale toward a great result.

> **VOCABULARY**
>
> *mitigation documents (n):* Any paperwork that makes you look responsible, reliable, valuable to the community, ambitious, or trustworthy.

The goal of the good guy / good gal packet is to protect the prosecutor from being criticized (or fired) for making a lenient plea offer or dismissal. The packet should include four types of mitigation documents:

1. Proof of what you have accomplished in the past

This includes letters of recommendation, awards, proof of employment, and past accomplishments.

2. Proof of who you are trying to be in the future

This includes documents that prove you are making progress toward future goals: for example, an application to school, an updated résumé, or proof of acceptance into some type of program or certification.

3. Proof that you've taken responsibility for the situation

This includes any counseling classes or sessions that you have completed, community service, and anything else that you've done that suggests you have learned your lesson and don't need more punishment.

4. Proof of medical treatment

This includes any medical treatment you have received in the past or are scheduled to receive that would be relevant to your case.

THE DEFENDANT'S GUIDE TO DEFENSE

> **REMEMBER**
>
> This is a competition: You vs. everyone else who has been arrested for the same thing. You need to build a better good guy / good gal packet than everyone else. The prosecutor will (subconsciously) compare your mitigation packet against every other one they have seen in their career.

Will the prosecutor be interested in what I do for a living?

Yes. They will, however, be especially interested in your plans to get a promotion or a better job. Show the prosecutors that you are using this situation as motivation to advance your career.

What else might the prosecutor be interested in?

Anything positive can potentially be useful! What is the most interesting thing about you? What is the most unique or strange thing that you've done? Was it amusing or charitable?

Prosecutors handle hundreds of cases at any given time. They rarely remember details about specific defendants. It can be beneficial to show the prosecutor something unique, even if it is irrelevant to the actual case, so that they will remember you and your case each time they talk with your defense attorney.

For example, did you get married in a *Star Wars* costume? Did you win a sandcastle building contest? Are you an artist? Have you ever been discussed in the media? Any positive media attention (even from a long time ago) can be useful in plea negotiations. Have you got an interesting event coming up? Give your attorney a picture, screenshot, or any document that would distinguish you from other defendants. If your attorney doesn't think the item will be helpful, they won't show it to the prosecutor. Even a small chance that it could be useful makes it worth the effort to send it to your attorney.

> **IMPORTANT**
>
> Sharing your hobby or pastime with the prosecutor is a useful technique to get them to relate to you. In general, prosecutors believe that the more time-consuming interests you have outside of work, the less likely you are to get in trouble again.

Will the prosecutors take into account that I could lose my job if convicted?

If you are able to show that a conviction will have a catastrophic impact on your career, it may help the defense attorney negotiate a non-conviction resolution. Gather any documents that explain the consequences of a conviction and give them to your defense attorney.

For example, this documentation could include the following:

1. The section of the human resource manual that outlines the consequences of an arrest or conviction

2. A letter from your boss describing the negative consequences of a conviction on your continued employment

Just because there are severe consequences to your career does not mean the prosecutors will automatically be lenient, though. They will consider how it impacts your job, but their position will depend on the facts of the case.

What if I am considering a new job that would likely be affected by a conviction?

The prosecutors will consider the consequences of a conviction only if you are currently working in, or actively pursuing, the job that would be jeopardized. The prosecutors will not care that you are "thinking" about becoming a nurse or doctor in the future. The good news is that a criminal case takes long enough for you to take concrete steps toward obtaining a new position. Give your attorney documents that show the steps you have taken.

I understand that it may be difficult to take steps toward a potential job when you don't know the outcome of your case (and whether you would fail a background check), but in my experience it is worth the risk. Even if you get stuck with a conviction, many companies will often overlook a criminal history if they are impressed with the job applicant.

■ COUNSELING

The most effective way to convince the prosecutor that you have learned your lesson is to complete a counseling class related to the arrest.

Most larger counties have classes designed for people charged with assault, theft, DWI/DUI, and drug-related offenses. In general, the classes cover the underlying issues related to the charge—for example, problems with anger, decision-making, drinking, or addiction—and offer alternative strategies for dealing with the situation in the future. Your attorney should know if there is a counseling class for your type of arrest. If so, you should take it as soon as possible.

At the end of the class, the instructor will give you a certificate proving that you completed the course. Take a photo of the certificate and email it to your defense attorney.

> **IMPORTANT**
>
> Taking a counseling class is not considered an admission of your guilt. The prosecutors will never say, "Aha! He took a class! He knows he is guilty!" Instead, they will be impressed.

If your defense attorney recommends that you take a class, you should take it regardless of whether you think you need it. There are two reasons for this. First, you may unexpectedly learn something from the class. And second, completing the class is valuable in plea negotiations.

Do not wait until the last moment to sign up for a class, though. Counseling services do not always have room for people on short notice. Your defense attorney should be sharing your accomplishments with the prosecutor, not the reasons why you haven't gotten something done.

The prosecutor will assume that if you don't have the skills to arrange your schedule to take a few classes, you won't be able to stay out of trouble in the future. Ironically, they will be even more convinced that you need to take a class.

Ask your friends and family for help if you're having trouble fitting it into your schedule. You may be surprised how willing they are to assist you.

What if there are no classes for what I'm charged with?

Some types of criminal charges don't have classes specifically designed for them. For example, there won't be a counseling class designed for "Harboring a Runaway Child" or "Fleeing a Police Officer." The best (and only) strategy in this situation is to find a private counselor instead. This is easily done by searching the internet.

> **HINT**
>
> Google "[hometown] counselor" or "[hometown] therapist" or "[hometown] psychiatrist."

When you discuss your goals with the private counselor, let them know that your defense attorney would like a short memo on letterhead at some point in the near future that includes this information:

- Confirmation that you met with the counselor
- How often you met with them
- A general description of what was discussed
- How seriously you appeared to take the counseling

If your counselor is unsure of what the letter should address, have them call your defense attorney.

Remember, you'll need to discuss the criminal case with the counselor at least once before he or she writes a letter on your behalf. After you've done that, however, you can talk about whatever you want—relationships, work, future goals. Do not be resistant to the idea of talking to a professional counselor! It can be surprisingly enjoyable.

> **IMPORTANT**
>
> Do you have insurance that would cover a therapist? Even if you have to pay out of pocket, counseling could be incredibly valuable for both you personally and the criminal case.

Can I take an online class?

Ask your attorney. However, prosecutors generally prefer an in-person class because they know that online courses don't require as much of your attention and participation. Your attorney will tell you which classes are acceptable to the prosecutors in your city or county.

■ SCHOOL GRADES

If you are still in school (or recently graduated), it is often useful to give your attorney a transcript of your grades and a schedule of your upcoming classes (if any). Prosecutors love to look at school transcripts because it breaks up the monotony of looking at offense reports.

Here's the good news: if you are still in school, the average length of a criminal case (six to ten months) gives you the opportunity to get in another round of grades. By improving your grades after the arrest, you can show the prosecutor that you have gotten your life back on the right track.

If you are not currently in school, it's worth thinking about signing up for an education program that fits your life goals. Being in school (even in an online program) is something that the prosecutors will consider when evaluating your case.

■ COMMUNITY SERVICE

Completing voluntary community service (before it is required by the prosecutor) is a great way to show that you are the type of person who accepts responsibility and can learn from your mistakes. Here are three reasons why:

- The prosecutor will assume that you thought about the arrest while doing the community service.
- It shows you take responsibility for your actions.
- The prosecutor will feel like you've already been somewhat punished.

Ask your attorney if doing community service would help your case and whether the court has a list of approved community service locations. If they don't, you can choose any nonreligious nonprofit organization.

It may surprise you, but some community service activities are enjoyable. If you are having fun, the time will fly by.

LETTERS OF RECOMMENDATION

Your defense attorney probably does not know you on a personal level. This makes it difficult for them to discuss your character with the prosecutor. This is why letters of recommendation are so valuable.

How do I ask someone for a letter of recommendation?

You should simply ask, "Would you mind writing me a character reference?" You do not need to tell the person why you are asking for the letter.

What makes for a good letter of recommendation?

1. The letter should be from the most impressive person who knows you well. The higher the title of the person, the more impactful the letter will be on the prosecutor. The best recommendation

letters are from current or former bosses, teachers, community leaders, and people you have helped in the past. Letters from family members can occasionally be valuable, but the prosecutor will give them less weight than letters from more objective parties.

2. The letter should explain how the writer knows you and give examples of things like your honesty, integrity, hard work, reliability, background, or any specific instances where you have excelled in a task. The letter does not have to mention your arrest specifically.

3. The letter should include the writer's contact information. The prosecutor is unlikely to contact them, but they want to be able to do so if necessary. Also, it looks suspicious if there is no contact info on the letter.

4. Ideally, the letter should be on letterhead, dated, and signed. However, the prosecutor will accept a letter in any format as long as they believe that it is authentic. A picture or scan of the letter is also acceptable. As a last resort, an email directly to your defense attorney will also work.

5. The letter should be addressed "To whom it may concern." It does not need to be addressed to a specific prosecutor, court, or judge—but it is acceptable if it is.

6. The ideal letter is three to four paragraphs in length, but it can be longer if necessary to communicate the quality of your character.

7. The letter does not need to mention the arrest. In fact, it is usually better if it doesn't.

8. If the letter does mention the arrest, it should not ask the prosecutor to dismiss the case or be lenient on you. The prosecutor will already assume that anyone who is vouching for your character would prefer the least amount of punishment possible.
9. You do not need to get more than three letters. Prosecutors don't have time to read more than a few per defendant. If you do get more, your attorney will choose the best ones to actually use.

> **IMPORTANT**
>
> Your defense attorney will review the letters before giving them to the prosecutor. If there is anything that the defense attorney doesn't like (or thinks could be improved), they will ask for a revised version.

■ MEDICAL RECORDS

In general, the prosecutors will view your medical issues with skepticism—because they don't like excuses for unlawful behavior. However, occasionally they will be sympathetic and allow the medical information to influence their opinion on your case. Ask your attorney if proof of any medical issues would be relevant and useful in your defense. Remember, the prosecutor will expect you to be actively working to improve your condition so the situation that led to your arrest doesn't happen again.

> **IMPORTANT**
>
> Just claiming to have medical issues is not sufficient. The prosecutor will require medical documentation that has your name, date, and a description of the condition in it. Sometimes a receipt from a hospital will have all the information. In other cases, a letter from a doctor will be necessary.

There are two types of medical issues that can be useful in a criminal case:

1. Medical issues that impact your physical condition and are directly related to the arrest. For example, if you are charged with DWI/DUI, any medical

condition that affects your coordination, eyesight, or metabolism may be relevant.
2. Medical issues that cause stress and could impact your decision-making.

Let your defense attorney know about any significant medical issues that you are dealing with (or have dealt with in the past). Your attorney will determine whether they will be useful to mention during plea negotiations.

> **I'm having trouble getting my medical records. Can my defense attorney help?**

Unfortunately, no. It is not any easier for your attorney to get copies of your medical records. Be persistent and don't give up! You are entitled to your own records.

YOUR VERSION OF THE ARREST

Your defense attorney usually gets the majority of the information about the arrest from the offense report. However, the police are not always accurate in their description of the event. Ask your attorney if they would like you to write down what happened from your perspective. If they say yes, show the document only to them.

Should I give my defense attorney a list of everyone who has information about the arrest?

Yes. You should provide your attorney with the contact information of anyone who has helpful information about the circumstances surrounding the arrest.

> **IMPORTANT**
>
> Never pressure a witness to say or do anything. This is a crime. If there is a question about whether the witness wants to help, let your defense attorney contact them instead of you.

Should I write a personal essay about my life?

Absolutely! This can be very useful for the defense attorney in negotiations with the prosecutor. Mention the key points in your life, the good and bad. Be careful not to blame other people or circumstances too much. Make sure it concludes with the goals you have set for yourself and your plans to accomplish them.

CHAPTER 5

THE BEST RESULT

Dismissal, Plea Bargain, or Jury Trial?

After you have set goals, made plans, put in the hard work, and provided your attorney with documentation, your attorney will negotiate with the prosecutor. Hopefully the result is some form of dismissal, or, if not, a compromise that involves minimal punishment. Once the negotiation is complete, you will decide whether to accept the offer or have a jury trial.

Let's first discuss what I know you are hoping for . . .

DISMISSAL: THE BEST POSSIBLE OUTCOME

At the start of any criminal case, your defense attorney's primary goal is to get the case dismissed. This is the best possible outcome because it means that the government has decided not to proceed with the charge (or charges) against you.

When considering a dismissal, the prosecutor will factor in the following conditions:

- Whether you have been in trouble before
- Whether the alleged offense was dangerous
- Whether there is a victim, and if they are upset
- Whether the evidence against you is weak or strong
- Whether you have done anything positive while the case is pending

A dismissal is the ideal result because, in most situations, you will have the option of having the charges expunged—deleted from your record. Ask your attorney if and when this would be possible.

> **IMPORTANT**
>
> There is no incentive for the prosecutor to dismiss a case quickly. They will be methodical and cautious when considering a dismissal.

Is it easy for the prosecutor to dismiss a case?

No. A prosecutor won't dismiss a case without thinking very carefully about every aspect of the arrest. They are cautious for a couple of reasons:

1. They worry that a dismissal might not dissuade you from repeating the alleged behavior.
2. They want to warn future employers, landlords, and the public in general that you have not always followed the rules.

How can you overcome these concerns? Your defense attorney can provide the prosecutor with a good guy / good gal packet that suggests you won't get in trouble again.

> **IMPORTANT**
>
> Your defense attorney can't *prove* what you will or won't do in the future. All they can do is offer evidence that suggests how you will behave after the case is over.

I didn't do it! Why hasn't my case been dismissed?

An innocent client makes the case harder! The prosecutor won't believe you are innocent without some convincing proof. And you, understandably, won't want to do anything to help get your case dismissed because you didn't do anything wrong. A case where the defendant claims total innocence is difficult to resolve.

> **IMPORTANT**
>
> If you accept no responsibility for the arrest, it can be hard to do the things that will minimize the consequences.

OK, I did it. But I still don't want to be punished too much.

Your attorney will always try to minimize the punishment, even if you are guilty.

They spelled my name wrong. Will my case be thrown out?

No. Clerical errors almost never impact the outcome of a criminal case. Be sure to point out anything that is wrong in the paperwork to your defense attorney in case there is some advantage you can gain, but don't expect it to make a difference.

Will they dismiss my case if it's my first offense?

While it certainly helps if this is the first time you've been arrested, that does not automatically mean it will be dismissed. A prosecutor will always review the circumstances of the arrest before considering a dismissal.

Will I have to do things to get my case dismissed?

Almost certainly. Prosecutors rarely dismiss a case without requiring at least something from the defendant. Of course, you can refuse to do what they want you to do. However, they will likely withdraw the offer to dismiss the case.

Is there *always* a way to get a case dismissed?

No. Sometimes nothing can convince the prosecutor to dismiss your case. You could win a Nobel Prize, and they would not change their mind. Of course, you don't have to accept the prosecutor's position. You have the right to have a jury trial.

■ PLEA BARGAINS

A plea bargain is a compromise between you and the government (represented by the prosecutor) that saves the time, resources, and risk of a jury trial. Without plea bargains, there would be too many jury trials for any courthouse to handle.

> **IMPORTANT**
>
> A plea bargain is the prosecutor asking, "Will you accept this punishment, instead of having a jury trial?" Implied in their question is the fact that they will ask for more punishment (than they offered in the plea bargain) if you lose the trial.

How does the prosecutor decide the terms of the plea bargain?

The prosecutor will compare the facts of your case with similar cases they have prosecuted over the years. They will look at five basic elements:

1. The type of crime
2. The minimum and maximum punishment allowable by law
3. The circumstances of the arrest
4. The amount of evidence of your guilt
5. Your criminal history

> **IMPORTANT**
>
> A prosecutor is unlikely to get in trouble for being tough on you, but they can certainly get in trouble for *going too easy*. If the plea bargain offer is lenient without a justifiable reason, the prosecutor might get disciplined, overlooked for promotion, or even fired.

How does the type of crime affect the plea bargain?

The prosecutor will be much more concerned about violent or dangerous crimes. For example, if the crime involves an injury or threat to another person, the prosecutor will feel more of a responsibility to seek a conviction. This is because the prosecutor believes that a conviction is more likely to convince you not to commit the crime again.

How will the circumstances of the arrest affect the plea bargain?

The prosecutor will always consider the details of the arrest—where it took place, who was involved, why you appeared to have committed the crime, and how you acted when you were arrested—before deciding what plea bargain to offer. Not all cases are treated the same, even if they are the same level of crime. For example, a theft charge might be any of the following:

- A homeless veteran stealing $100 worth of food from a grocery store
- A suburban mom shoplifting $100 worth of jewelry
- A store employee stealing $100 from the cash register

In most jurisdictions, these crimes would be charged at the same level based on the value of the stolen property. However, the prosecutor will likely feel more determined to convict the employee who is stealing, in order to warn potential future employers. In fact, a conviction is sometimes more important to the prosecutor than actual punishment because a conviction can be seen on future background checks.

How does the amount of evidence impact the plea bargain offer?

In general, the more evidence of your guilt that the prosecutor possesses, the less likely they are to offer a lenient plea bargain. For example, if there are two eyewitnesses, a video, and your fingerprints, and you admitted to the crime, the prosecutor will likely start by offering a tough plea bargain. This is because the prosecutor will feel like you don't have much choice but to accept the plea bargain (because you would probably lose a trial). On the other hand, if the evidence is considered weak (e.g., there is only one semi-credible witness), the prosecutor may be inclined to make a better offer in order to persuade you not to have a trial.

Does the prosecutor want to have a trial?

Probably not. The prosecutor would prefer that you accept a plea bargain because it is quick, efficient, and doesn't require the participation of all of the people necessary for a jury trial (jury members, court reporter, multiple prosecutors, judge, witnesses, victim, etc.). Your defense attorney will use this to your advantage during negotiations.

What about the presumption of innocence?

If you are disappointed with the plea bargain offer, you might wonder, "What happened to the presumption of innocence? Do the prosecutors just assume I'm guilty?"

Well, to be blunt, the answer is yes. A prosecutor rarely considers the possibility that you are innocent. They will generally assume that whatever the police wrote in the offense report is true. This does not mean that they can't be convinced that you are innocent with some strong contradictory evidence, but the prosecutor will certainly begin with the assumption that you are guilty.

The presumption of innocence only applies when you reject the plea bargain and choose to have a trial. At the beginning of a trial the judge will tell the jury to start with the belief that you are innocent.

Will my behavior after I was arrested be used against me?

The prosecutor will definitely take any disrespectful behavior toward the police into consideration when deciding how to handle the case. If you were rude to the police, the police likely included a description of what you did in the offense report. If the prosecutors happen to learn of anything else negative that you have done since the arrest, they will certainly hold this against you as well.

How do prior arrests affect my case?

The prosecutor will always look at your criminal history before deciding what type of plea bargain to offer. Any prior arrests, *even if they were dismissed*, will be taken into consideration.

Why would they hold an old dismissed case against me?

The prosecutor on your new case will likely have no idea why the old case was dismissed. They will always suspect that you were at least somewhat culpable.

Is it bad if I've been arrested for the same thing before?

Yes. If you have been arrested for the same thing in the past, the prosecutor will likely insist on harsher punishment than you received on the older case. Prosecutors generally operate on the theory that if you commit the same crime again, you weren't punished sufficiently the first time.

What happens if I get arrested again while this case is still going on?

The prosecutor and judge will conclude that you are reckless and potentially dangerous to the community. They will likely insist on a conviction on both the old and new case—which could include jail time. Their goal would be to get your attention and increase the chance that you decide to follow the rules in the future.

Do not do anything that risks a second arrest while your case is pending! Any progress that your attorney made on the first case will disappear in an instant.

HINT

If you accidentally violate a rule of court, instead of making an excuse, say, "It won't happen again." This is what everyone in the criminal justice system really wants to hear. Also, make sure it doesn't actually happen again.

What if the facts of my case are pretty bad?

There are some cases where the prosecutor will *insist* on a conviction: for example, if someone got hurt, if a weapon was involved, if you've been in trouble before, or if the prosecutor suspects only a conviction will convince you to follow the rules in the future.

In these circumstances, it is likely that nothing will change the prosecutor's mind. This won't stop your defense attorney from exploring every possible angle and looking for any path to get an extraordinary result, but it is important to understand that some cases are impossible to get dismissed. However, even if you can't get your case dismissed, all of the good things you do while the case is pending could reduce the punishment significantly.

Will the prosecutor care that this case is making my life difficult?

The prosecutor will not care too much. In fact, they will likely think a little hardship will help you remember the consequences of violating the rules.

> **IMPORTANT**
>
> There is an element of tough love to the criminal justice system. It can feel like the prosecutor or judge is punishing you when, in fact, they are trying to help convince you to make better decisions in the future.

Doesn't everyone in the system just want to make money?

No. It certainly can *feel* like everyone is after your money because there are so many fines, expenses, and costs throughout the process, but the reality is that *it is expensive to maintain the criminal justice system*. Taxpayers generally want some of the expenses to be covered by the people who have been arrested.

There is another reason, though. Prosecutors often use fines as *negative reinforcement*—they want to discourage people from committing future crimes by creating financial consequences. While this may or may not work (depending on your personality and financial resources), it is not the same as trying to make money off of you.

What is probation?

Probation, sometimes called *community supervision*, is technically a jail sentence that is "suspended"—as long as you do not violate the rules of probation, you do not go to jail. The rules of probation will vary by state and county, but these are the basic concepts:

- You must visit your probation officer at regular intervals, usually every month.
- You must complete any tasks or counseling and pay any fees that are required in a timely manner. These are called the *terms* or *conditions* of probation.
- You cannot get arrested again during the period of probation. If you do, you will be in trouble for both the new charge and for violating your existing probation.
- You may not use alcohol or any drugs without a prescription.
- You must get approval to travel out of the county or state. As long as the travel is for a legitimate reason and you haven't given them any reason not to trust you, the probation officer or judge will likely give you permission.

What does the probation officer do?

Probation officers are in charge of making sure that you successfully complete the requirements of your probation. They are required to tell the judge if you break the rules.

The key to working with probation officers is to act happy that you are on probation. That sounds absurd, of course, but probation officers believe you *should* be happy to be on probation, because the alternative is going to jail.

Probation will be inconvenient. The scheduled visits and tasks will interfere with your regular life. If you act annoyed when you visit your probation officer, even just by sulking or acting passive-aggressively, the visit will be unpleasant. At some point, the judge may ask the probation officer about your case. It would be best if the probation officer has only good things to say about you.

> **What if the probation officer says I violated probation, but I didn't?**

You are entitled to have a hearing in front of the judge. The judge will decide whether you violated probation or not.

NEGOTIATING WITH THE PROSECUTOR

A plea bargain negotiation is not like an ordinary business transaction where either side can walk away (and never talk again) if they don't like the deal. A criminal case *must be resolved* with either a plea bargain or a legal battle. This adds pressure to the negotiation process on both sides.

When will my defense attorney start negotiating?

Your defense attorney will likely wait to begin negotiations until they have seen all of the evidence that the prosecutor possesses and received the most important mitigation documents from you.

What strategies are available to a defense attorney?

Every criminal case involves three elements that affect the outcome: the evidence, the defendant, and the law. Your defense attorney's plan will be to explore all three elements to improve the chance of getting a good result in your case.

1. **The evidence (facts of the case).** Your defense attorney will attempt to convince the prosecutor that you are innocent or that the facts of the case are not as bad as the police officer reported them to be. This is primarily done by finding contradictory evidence, interviewing witnesses, taking pictures of the scene, and gathering documents that disprove an allegation.
2. **The defendant (you).** Your defense attorney will try to convince the prosecutor that you are not the

type of person who is likely to get in trouble again. This is an area where you can contribute the most. You should complete any tasks that your attorney suggests, make some ambitious life goals, and provide any requested documentation as soon as possible.

3. **The law.** Your defense attorney will carefully examine the law and attempt to convince the prosecutor or judge that your case should be thrown out due to a constitutional violation, or, at the very least, that there is a legal issue that should be taken into consideration. This is what your attorney learned how to do in law school. It should be noted that discovering a legal issue that gets the case thrown out is rare. It generally only happens when the defense attorney uncovers a major mistake made by the police.

How many times will my defense attorney negotiate with the prosecutor?

It depends. It can be ten times or more! Sometimes cases are resolved quickly, and other times they drag on for a long time.

> **IMPORTANT**
>
> Good results take time because the court system moves slowly. You should be patient. Like you, your defense attorney wants the best result as soon as possible.

What happens if my defense attorney asks for a better plea bargain without new information or mitigation documents?

If the prosecutor sees from their notes that nothing has changed since the last court date, they will probably not significantly change or improve the current plea bargain offer. The best strategy is to come back with more mitigation documents on each court date.

What does a defense attorney think about after negotiating with a prosecutor?

Your attorney will try to figure out if something else can be done to get an even better result. Did the prosecutor's voice sound firm? What fact about the case was the prosecutor hung up on? If your attorney thinks there is any chance for a better plea bargain offer down the road, he or she will reset the case and come back and try again.

How can the negotiation positions change while the case is pending?

As your case moves through the system, the negotiating position of your attorney and the prosecutor can shift due to events that happen in between court dates.

Hopefully your position improves over time. This can happen in many different ways, including the following scenarios:

1. Your defense attorney provides additional mitigating documents to the prosecutor that convince them to be more lenient.
2. Favorable evidence is discovered (or finally looked at) by the prosecutor, and your guilt becomes less clear to them.
3. Other people involved in the offense (witnesses, victims, etc.) lose interest in the case, stop communicating with the prosecutor, or become less credible for some reason.
4. The police officer who arrested you gets fired or quits. This won't make the case go away automatically, but it definitely helps.
5. The prosecutor gets pressured by their boss or the judge to resolve your case, and they significantly improve the plea bargain offer. This can happen if the court's docket gets too large and the

prosecutor's office begins to look for easy cases to resolve.
6. The prosecutor loses interest in your case and is more willing to compromise. This can happen if they get busy with new cases or there is an upcoming trial on another case.
7. The first prosecutor is reassigned, and the new one doesn't want to spend the energy to learn about your case.

However, sometimes your position can get *worse* as time passes. This can happen for different reasons:

1. You get arrested on another charge.
2. You do not comply with the conditions of your bond.
3. You don't do anything while the case is pending, making it look like you aren't taking things seriously.
4. More evidence is discovered that confirms your guilt.
5. Evidence of other crimes you may have committed is discovered, such as criminal cases in other counties or states.
6. A new prosecutor gets assigned to the case and is more determined to punish you than the first prosecutor was.

Your defense attorney will determine whether anything has changed since the last time he or she discussed your case with the prosecutor and decide whether to push for a quick resolution or to delay so that you can complete more tasks and gather more mitigation documents.

What is the ideal negotiation position?

The best position is to have a lot of mitigation documents—a good guy / good gal packet—and a valid legal issue that makes the prosecutor less confident about their case against you. Only one of those things (the mitigation documents) is in your control.

I have a good explanation for what happened. Why won't the prosecutor believe me?

It can be hard to understand why your story won't convince the prosecutor to dismiss your case. More than likely, it's for one of these reasons:

1. You're not the first person to tell them the same story—and the other people were lying. Because so many people have lied in the past, the prosecutors will assume that you aren't telling the truth either. It's like saying the dog ate your homework. Even if it is true, you're going to have a hard time finding someone who will believe you.
2. Your story has gaps and doesn't completely disprove the accusations you are facing. All prosecutors are trained to find holes in the stories they are told by the defense attorneys. The prosecutors are not going to be fooled by a half-true story.

> **IMPORTANT**
>
> A good plan is better than a great excuse. The prosecutor wants to hear that you've got a satisfactory plan to address whatever issues led to the arrest in the first place. Better yet, the prosecutor wants to hear that you've already started the plan or, even better, that it's been completed.

Will the plea bargain allow me to eventually clear my record?

Ask your attorney if successful completion of the plea bargain would make you eligible to expunge, seal, or clear your record. If so, find out when you would be eligible and put the date in your calendar. In nearly all situations, you will need to hire an attorney to do the extra legal work required to clear your record. The process is not likely to be automatic.

Should I be satisfied with the plea bargain? Or should I turn it down and have a jury trial?

This is the most important question you will have to consider during this entire process. Before you make a decision, your defense attorney will advise you on the strength or weakness of the evidence against you. If the prosecutor has significant evidence that you are guilty, then your attorney will likely say that a jury trial is not a good idea. If they don't have strong evidence, then your attorney will discuss the pros and cons of having a trial. Ultimately, you must rely on your defense attorney's experience and opinion to help make the decision that is best for you given the specific circumstances of your case.

IMPORTANT

Sometimes a jury will acquit a defendant even when there is a lot of evidence of guilt. Other times a jury will convict with very little evidence of guilt. Even the most experienced defense attorney cannot predict what a jury will do.

Can I ask for a second opinion from another defense attorney?

You can try. However, attorneys are ethically prohibited from discussing a case with a person that they know is represented by another attorney (without permission from the other attorney). This, in addition to being careful about not stepping on their colleague's toes, will usually make other attorneys reluctant to get involved in your case if you already have an attorney.

Can a defense attorney convince the prosecutor that the police made a mistake?

Occasionally, but the default attitude of the prosecutor is that the police did not make a mistake. This is because, unlike the prosecutor, the police were at the scene, talking to witnesses, interpreting the environment (such as the smells and weather conditions), and observing the body language of the people involved.

Of course, an experienced prosecutor will consider the *possibility* that the police made a mistake. However, unless there is some *evidence* that the police got it wrong, it is unlikely that a prosecutor will question the officer's conclusions.

That does not mean that it is impossible to convince the prosecutor that the police got the wrong person. It just isn't easy. Often the prosecutors will say, "Just put it on the jury docket." Your defense attorney may be happy to do that, or they may be worried that a jury won't believe you are not guilty either.

Defense attorney: My client is innocent. We want the case dismissed right away.
Prosecutor: The officer says he saw your client commit the crime.
Defense attorney: The officer is mistaken.
Prosecutor: Sounds like you need to have a jury trial.

> **IMPORTANT**
>
> The prosecutor will not believe that you are innocent just because your defense attorney tells them that you are. Your attorney will need to provide evidence. Of course, if you have a trial, it is the other way around. The prosecutor would have to provide evidence of your guilt.

Can you give an example of how mitigation documents work in negotiations?

Sure. Consider the following scene: The defense attorney sits across the table from the prosecutor. The prosecutor reads the offense report, checks the criminal history of the defendant, and makes a note in the file. Compare the two negotiations.

Negotiation #1

Prosecutor: Looks like your client got caught red-handed. What's he been doing since the arrest?
Defense attorney: Not sure.
Prosecutor: Where does he work?
Defense attorney: I think he does something for a car rental company.
Prosecutor: Did he take the counseling class?
Defense attorney: Maybe? He hasn't given me anything, though.
Prosecutor: How about two years of probation, a $1,000 fine, a hundred hours of community service, and counseling?
Defense attorney: OK. I'll ask him if he wants to accept the deal.

Negotiation #2

Prosecutor: Looks like your client got caught red-handed.

Defense attorney: Perhaps, but since the arrest he's completed twenty hours of community service.

Prosecutor: Where did he do the community service?

Defense attorney: At the animal shelter. Here's the proof. He's also enrolled in a software coding program that starts next month. Here's a receipt for the class.

Prosecutor: Why was he stealing?

Defense attorney: He was having trouble with his parents. But he's serious about changing his life. Look, he's also completed a twelve-hour theft class. Here's the certificate. And here's a letter from his parents describing how hard he's working to turn his life around. How about some form of dismissal with a $500 fine and private counseling?

Prosecutor: Let me think about that. Where does he work?

Defense attorney: He just got a job at a car rental company. Here's a letter from his boss describing how valuable an employee he is.

Prosecutor: OK. Have him do a little more community service, and I'll consider a dismissal with a fine.

Defense attorney: Great. I'll reset the case to give him time to do the extra community service.

I can't guarantee how the plea bargain negotiation will go in your case. But I do know that if your attorney can describe your accomplishments and prove how hard you've been working (thanks to the mitigation documents that you provide), he or she will have a better chance at getting a good result.

Will the prosecutor ever get mad at the defense attorney for asking for a better deal?

Sometimes the prosecutor will signal that they're done negotiating by announcing, "That's as far as I can go on these facts" or "That's my bottom line." A good defense attorney will know when it is a waste of time to continue pushing for a better result.

When the defense and prosecution are at an impasse—where neither side can compromise any more than they already have and there is nothing more that you can do to change the prosecutor's mind—you and your attorney will decide whether to accept the current plea bargain offer or have a jury trial.

VOCABULARY

bottom line (n): The lowest amount of punishment that the prosecutor is willing to agree to on the case.

Can a criminal case go on forever?

No. Eventually, the judge will refuse to give either side another court setting to continue plea bargain negotiations. This means that the case has nowhere to go but the plea docket or the jury docket. This forces both sides to come to an agreement quickly or get ready for a jury trial.

> **VOCABULARY**
>
> *plea docket (n):* A type of court setting where the terms of the plea bargain have been agreed to by both sides. Often a case is put on the plea docket because the defendant needs to complete tasks before the deal can be completed.

■ JURY TRIAL

When you have a pending case, it can feel like you are at the mercy of the judge, prosecutor, and police. However, the ultimate power is really yours: the right to have a jury trial. You can refuse to accept the plea bargain and insist on letting your fellow citizens decide whether you are guilty or not (and what the punishment should be).

Of course, having a jury trial is like gambling. You risk more punishment on the hope that you are acquitted—found not guilty—and therefore receive no punishment at all. Some people have no problem gambling, and others don't like the idea at all.

During my career as a defense attorney, I've helped my clients decide whether to accept the plea bargain or have a jury trial thousands of times. We have long discussions, either in my office or outside the courtroom, about the risks of a trial, their plans for the future, and how their decision might impact those plans. It is never an easy decision. However, once the pros and cons are identified, the right answer is fairly obvious in most instances.

What is the jury docket?

When you have rejected the best plea bargain that the prosecutor is willing to offer, your attorney will inform the judge that the case needs to be placed on the jury docket—a court date for cases that require a trial.

The court will likely have many cases set on the jury docket on a particular day. Sometimes as many as fifty! The judge decides which case goes to trial on that day. Your attorney may know in advance that your case has been chosen, or you might not know whether you will have a trial until the morning of your court date. It is important to note that only one case can go to trial (unless there are other judges and courtrooms available). What happens to all the other cases set on the jury docket? They either get reset for the next jury setting, or the defense attorney and prosecutor work out some type of plea bargain.

When deciding which case to try (i.e., to bring to trial), the judge will take into consideration which witnesses are available. For example, if the arresting officer is unavailable, or the defense has an expert witness that cannot be in court, then the judge will likely choose a different case in which all the witnesses are available.

The judge will also usually give preference to older cases because it becomes harder to have a fair trial when a long time has passed since the arrest (e.g., witnesses move, memories fade).

What questions should I ask my attorney about a jury trial?

The primary question is "What is the worst punishment that could happen if we lose?" Your attorney may say that the potential punishment is far worse than the plea bargain. For example, losing a trial could result in jail time. Is this something you would be willing to risk? Some people would be willing to risk it, and others would not. In other situations, your attorney may say that losing a jury trial would not result in much worse punishment than the prosecutors are currently offering in the plea bargain. If you don't have much to lose, maybe you wouldn't mind rolling the dice and seeing what happens. Deciding whether to have a jury trial is usually a very difficult decision. Even experienced defense attorneys can only offer guidance. They will help you make a decision, but they can't make the decision for you.

What evidence will the jury hear?

This is an important question to ask your attorney. A jury trial is not like a regular argument between people (where you can say anything you want). A judge will only allow the jury to hear evidence that is relevant to the crime. This means that excuses and justifications for behavior may not be allowed to be talked about. When trying to figure out if you have a chance to win a trial, you need to know what information the jury will be allowed to hear.

Will a prosecutor try hard to win a jury trial?

Yes. The prosecutor will try very hard to win. They do not like to lose.

What are the possible outcomes of a jury trial?

When comparing your potential punishment (after having a trial) to the plea bargain, there are four possibilities:

1. You are found guilty, and the sentence is worse than the plea bargain offer.

2. You are found guilty, and the sentence is the same as the plea bargain offer.
3. You are found guilty, and the sentence is better than the plea bargain offer.
4. You are found not guilty.

Your attorney will be able to explain the possible results of a trial in more detail.

> **VOCABULARY**
>
> *sentence (n):* The punishment ordered by the judge or jury.

WHEN THE CASE IS (FINALLY) OVER

When your case is finally over, it will feel like school is out for the summer. It is a great feeling! Most people are emotionally exhausted from dealing with all the requirements. Hopefully you will be satisfied with the result of the case and have made some improvements to your life. I also hope that you had a great defense attorney. If so, make sure you express your appreciation. Being a defense attorney is a tough job, and not all clients realize how hard their attorney worked for them (and how much worse the punishment could've been with a less capable attorney). And you won't hurt your attorney's feelings if you say, "No offense, but I hope this is the last time I have to talk with you!" They've all heard that sentiment many times and will almost certainly reply, with a smile, "Yes, me too."

CHAPTER 6

Now Is the Perfect Time

I hope that this book has made the criminal justice system a little easier to understand and deal with. Regardless of how your case turns out, hopefully this book has convinced you that a misdemeanor arrest is the perfect opportunity for you to discover new skills, create better relationships, and generally improve your life. Your hard work in these areas will directly benefit your case. I really believe that. As one of my clients recently said, "The arrest was the *best* worst thing that has ever happened to me."

Where should you start? There are thousands of books in the self-help genre that will give you advice on strategies for improving the quality of your life. I highly encourage you to find an author that you can relate to. You've got a goal, you've made the plan, and now it's time to do the work.

Here is a quick overview of nine areas of life that I believe hold great opportunities for self-improvement:

Organization

Figure out which aspects of your life need to be organized. Clean your house. Create a budget for your finances. Buy a new calendar app for your phone. The process of organizing your life can be a form of reinvention—you are figuring out who you want to be in the future.

Inspiration

This is the time to do some serious self-reflection. Read or listen to good books. Seek wisdom. Set an ambitious goal that motivates you. Maybe you would benefit from some time off? Or you could take a trip to somewhere you've always wanted to go.

Mentorship

This is a great opportunity to get advice from people you respect. You would be surprised at how many accomplished people love to share the wisdom they have gained through their life experience. Who do you know who might be willing to talk with you? Does anyone in your family know someone? Perhaps a local author, artist, or business leader would be willing to meet you for lunch or coffee?

Creativity

Focus your stress, anger, or sadness into art. Start drawing, painting, playing music, or writing. Take a beginner class in something you've always wanted to try. Convince a friend to join you. Start a journal. Reconnect with the time in your life when you enjoyed creating.

Friendship and Community

Contact an old friend. Find a new one. Have lunch or coffee with a colleague. Find an online group that shares your interests. Go to lectures.

Exploring Your Local History and Culture

Find something in your area that you haven't done. Are there any museums that you've never been to? A state park? A nature trail? A historic building? You never know what will inspire you.

Career

This is a good time to update your résumé. Take a free online course to improve your qualifications. Even if you aren't planning on looking for another job, the process of focusing on your skills could inspire you to consider new opportunities.

Health

Improving your health is the most effective method of improving the quality of your life. Join a gym. Buy a treadmill or a bicycle. Sign up for a sports league. Stop drinking alcohol. It is also a good time to switch to healthier foods.

Looking Inward

Examine why the incident happened in the first place. What type of pressure led to the arrest? Was it financial? Were you having relationship issues? Were you depressed? What is the best way to address that pressure? Seek a professional counselor.

> **IMPORTANT**
>
> You won't learn from a mistake if you can't admit you made one. Denying responsibility for your role in the arrest makes it difficult to do the self-reflection that is necessary to make positive changes in your life.

■ FINAL THOUGHTS

I'll leave you with a parable about someone else who got in trouble:

> A sixteen-year-old kid is driving a car in the early morning hours with his thirty-year-old ne'er-do-well uncle (who has been arrested many times) in the passenger seat.
>
> In the spirit of youthful recklessness, and with the encouragement of the uncle, the nephew drives the car onto the deserted public beach and starts spinning out, doing donuts in the sand. The nephew and uncle are both laughing and having a great time, but they both know that they should not be driving on the beach.

> Soon, the police arrive, park their cars, and three officers start walking in the sand toward the car. The officers do not look amused.
>
> The nephew, holding the steering wheel, starts to nervously shake. He begins to sob, worried about the consequences of his actions.
>
> The uncle, who has spent time in prison, puts his hand on the kid's knee and says, "Relax. I've seen trouble . . . and this ain't it."

Of course, I don't know what you are charged with or the impact it has had on your life, but there is a good chance that, in the grand scheme of things, this arrest will not ruin your future. It may be inconvenient and require you to make some lifestyle adjustments, but if you learn from this experience, the long-term consequences will likely be less painful than you originally imagined. In fact, this experience may be the wake-up call you needed. It could be a pivotal moment in your life.

Consider this: What if this is the last time you ever get in trouble? Dare I say it? Maybe the arrest was a good thing!

When the case is over, the things you will have learned about life, responsibility, human nature, criminal justice, and law enforcement will be incredibly valuable—not just for yourself, but also for your family and friends. It is my advice to look at this situation as the perfect opportunity to make the changes that will lead to a better result on your case and greater long-term happiness.

ABOUT THE AUTHOR

Photo © 2019 Courtney Cobelle

Charlie Roadman has been a criminal defense lawyer in Austin, Texas, for more than eighteen years. He received his law degree from the University of Texas School of Law and has dedicated his career to representing his clients with integrity, honesty, and clear communication. His philosophy is to fight every aspect of a charge, while providing guidance on ways to reduce the negative impacts on a client's life. Roadman views each case as an opportunity for a client to make positive life changes that can turn an unfortunate event into a personal success story.

Made in United States
Orlando, FL
22 May 2025